A TAPESTRY OF CULTURES

EXPLORING INDIA FROM KASHMIR TO KANYAKUMARI

DR. JAGADEESH PILLAI

Made with ♥ on the Notion Press Platform
www.notionpress.com

|| "Dedicated to all who seek to understand and appreciate Indian culture and tradition." ||

Contents

Contents

Prayer

**"Om Bhadram Karnebbhih Shrunuyaama
DevaahBhadram Pashyemaakshabhiryajatraah
SthirairangaistushtuvaamsastanoobhihVyashema
Devahitam YadaayuhSwasti Na Indro
VridhashravaahSwasti Nah Pooshaa
VishwavedaahSwasti Nastaarkshyo ArishtanemihSwasti
No Brihaspatir DadhaatuOm Shantih, Shantih, Shantih"**

The literal meaning of this mantra is: OM. O Gods! Let us hear auspicious words from our ears. O reverent Gods! Let us behold propitious visions from our eyes, let our organs and body be stable, healthy, and strong. Let us do that which is pleasing to the gods in the life span allotted to us. May Indra, inscribed in the scriptures, bring us fortune! May Pushan, the knower of the world, grant us prosperity! May Trakshya, who vanquishes enemies, bestow us with blessings! May Brihaspati bring us success!
OM Peace, Peace, Peace.

About The Author

Dr. Jagadeesh Pillai is a renowned Guinness World Record holder, writer, and researcher hailing from Varanasi, also known as the abode of Lord Shiva. With a Ph.D. in Vedic Science and a range of creative ideas and achievements, he is a true polymath. He is the author of more than 100 books including Research Publications. Although his roots can be traced back to Kerala, the people of Varanasi hold him in high regard and affectionately consider him one of their own.

Dr. Pillai has achieved four Guinness World Records in the following subjects:

"Script to Screen" - In this record, Dr. Pillai produced and directed an animation film within the shortest time possible, breaking the previous record set by Canadians. He has also received numerous national and international awards and recognitions for this achievement.

Longest Line of Postcards - For this record, Dr. Pillai created a line of 16,300 postcards on the occasion of the 163rd anniversary of Indian Postal Day. The event also included a questionnaire about the Indian flag.

Largest Poster Awareness Campaign - Dr. Pillai designed an awareness campaign on the subject of "Beti Bachao - Beti Padhao" (Save the Girl Child - Educate the Girl Child) to achieve this record.

Largest Envelope - In tribute to the Indian Prime Minister's

"Make in India" initiative, Dr. Pillai created a 4000 square meter envelope using waste paper to achieve this record.

Attempted - **70000 Candles on a 210 kg Cake** - To celebrate the 70th Indian Independence Day, Dr. Pillai attempted to light 70,000 candles on a 210 kg cake, which was recorded in World Records India.

Attempted - **Documentary on Dhamek Stupa of Sarnath in 17 Languages** - Dr. Pillai attempted to create a documentary on the Dhamek Stupa of Sarnath, dubbing it in 17 different languages. The result of this attempt is currently awaiting confirmation from the Guinness World Records.

Dr. Pillai is skilled in teaching the Bhagavad Gita, a Hindu scripture, and is popular among young people. He has helped many young people improve their lives through his motivational teachings.

In addition to teaching, he has composed and sung numerous Sanskrit Bhajans and patriotic songs.

He has also written and directed several short films and documentaries for awareness campaigns, and has volunteered with the police in both UP and Kerala to spread awareness about various issues through videos and photography.

Incredibly, he has produced and directed over 100 documentaries about the city of Varanasi, all on his own.

He has also helped and guided more than 25 boys and girls

to achieve world records through creative and innovative methods. He is a multifaceted person who uses his intellect and the blessings given to him by God to excel in various areas. He is both a teacher and a student, always learning and teaching, and is able to master any subject he comes across.

He is a selfless social activist and motivational speaker who has overcome struggles and failures to become a successful and enthusiastic individual with a rich life experience.

In addition to his work with the Bhagavad Gita, he is also an efficient Tarot card reader, Astro-Vastu consultant, and a talented singer and composer. He has sung the entire Ram Charita Manas and Bhagavad Gita in his own compositions, and has sung the phrase "Lokah Samastha Sukhino Bhavantu" in 50 different languages. He is currently working on a detailed and scientific study of Vedas, Upanishads, Puranas, and the Bhagavad Gita. He has also composed and sung the Hanuman Chalisa and Gayatri Mantra in 108 and 1008 different compositions, respectively.

Awards - Four Times Guinness World Records, Winner of Mahatma Gandhi Vishwa Shanti Puraskar, Mahatma Gandhi Global Peace Ambassador, Kashi Ratna Award, Dr. APJ Abdul Kalam Motivational Person of the Year 2017, Mother Teresa Award, Indira Gandhi Priyadarshini Award, Bharat Vikas Ratna Award, Udyog Ratna Award, Vigyan Prasar Award, Poorvanchal Ratn Samman.

Preface

"A Tapestry of Cultures: Exploring India from Kashmir to Kanyakumari" is a comprehensive guide that takes the reader on a journey through the diverse cultures, traditions, and heritage of India. Covering all 28 official states and 8 official Union Territories, this book offers a quick reference to the rich tapestry of cultures that make up this vibrant country. From the snow-capped peaks of Kashmir to the sun-drenched beaches of Kanyakumari, this book delves deep into the history, customs, and way of life of each state and Union Territory, providing a unique and in-depth understanding of the people, places, and traditions that make India such a fascinating and captivating destination. Whether you are an armchair traveler or an avid explorer, this book will give you a sense of visiting all the states and Union Territories of India, and leave you with a deeper appreciation of the country's rich cultural heritage.

"A Tapestry of Cultures: Exploring India from Kashmir to Kanyakumari" is an invaluable resource for anyone interested in learning more about the diverse and fascinating country of India. Each chapter of the book is dedicated to a different state or Union Territory, providing a detailed overview of its culture, traditions, heritage, and notable landmarks. From the bustling streets of Delhi to the tranquil backwaters of Kerala, the book covers a wide range of topics including art, architecture, music, cuisine, festivals, and more.

The book also highlights the unique customs and practices

of each state and Union Territory, providing readers with an in-depth understanding of the cultural fabric that makes India so rich and diverse. Whether you are an Indian national or an international traveler, this book will help you to appreciate the nuances of India's culture and heritage, and to understand the intricate tapestry of cultures that make up this incredible country.

With its detailed descriptions and beautiful photographs, "A Tapestry of Cultures: Exploring India from Kashmir to Kanyakumari" is a must-read for anyone interested in learning more about India. It will be an inspiring and enlightening read, and will give you a deeper appreciation of the country's rich cultural heritage.

28 STATES

States and Capitals per https://knowindia.india.gov.in/states-uts/

1. Andhra Pradesh(Amaravati)
2. Arunachal Pradesh(Itanagar)
3. Assam(Dispur)
4. Bihar(Patna)
5. Chhattisgarh(Raipur)
6. Goa(Panaji)
7. Gujarat(Gandhinagar)
8. Haryana(Chandigarh)
9. Himachal Pradesh(Shimla)
10. Jharkhand(Ranchi)
11. Karnataka(Bangalore)
12. Kerala(Thiruvananthapuram)
13. Madhya Pradesh(Bhopal)
14. Maharashtra(Mumbai)
15. Manipur(Imphal)
16. Meghalaya(Shillong)
17. Mizoram(Aizawl)
18. Nagaland(Kohima)
19. Odisha(Bhubaneshwar)
20. Punjab(Chandigarh)
21. Rajasthan(Jaipur)
22. Sikkim(Gangtok)
23. Tamil Nadu(Chennai)
24. Telangana(Hyderabad)
25. Tripura(Agartala)

26. Uttarakhand(Dehradun)
27. Uttar Pradesh(Lucknow)
28. West Bengal(Kolkata)

CHAPTER ONE

Andhra Pradesh

Andhra Pradesh is a state located in the southern region of India, known for its rich culture, traditions, and history. The state is home to diverse ethnic groups, each with their own unique customs, languages, and traditions.

The culture of Andhra Pradesh is heavily influenced by the Hindu religion, with many temples, festivals and rituals being an integral part of the state's culture. The state is known for its traditional dance forms, such as the Kuchipudi and the Lambadi, which showcase the state's rich cultural heritage. Andhra Pradesh is also known for its traditional handicrafts, including Kalamkari, Kondapalli toys and the famous Andhra Pradesh silk saris. The cuisine of Andhra Pradesh is characterized by its use of local herbs and spices, with popular dishes like biryani, dosa and Andhra-style pickles being enjoyed by locals and tourists alike.

The state is home to many important historical and religious sites, including the Tirupati Venkateswara Temple, the Sri Kalahasti Temple and the Araku Valley. Andhra Pradesh is also known for its natural beauty, with popular tourist destinations such as the Horsley Hills, the

Papi Kondalu and the Konaseema.

The official language of Andhra Pradesh is Telugu, while other languages spoken in the state include Hindi and English. The majority of the population follows Hinduism, but there is also a significant presence of Islam in the state.

Andhra Pradesh is a state that offers a unique blend of culture, traditions, and history. It is an ideal destination for those interested in exploring the diversity of India's culture, as well as for nature enthusiasts looking to explore the state's beautiful landscapes and natural wonders.

CHAPTER TWO

Arunachal Pradesh

The Indian state of Arunachal Pradesh is a multicultural mosaic of distinctive cultures and traditions, each unique in its own way. This land located in the northeast corner of India is a hotbed of exclusive practices, customs, languages, and places.

The people of Arunachal Pradesh are divided into various ethnic and tribal groups, with their own distinct cultural identities and special practices. These proud artistic communities include the Nyishi, Tangsa, Apatani, Nocte, Wancho, Tagin, Bugun,Sherdukpen, Adi and several others. Each group has its own language, food, clothing and ceremonial traditions.

The people of Arunachal attend festivals to honour various gods and celebrate various ceremonies including marriage, death, birth and harvest. The ancient Dree festival of the Apatani Khimyos is one of such festivals celebrated for four days in the first week of July. Traditional sports like hunting and fishing competitions, archery and swimmingare also organized during this event. The Nyokum Yullo festival celebrated by the Nyishi tribe is another important festival that marks a pageant of dance, colour, festive foods and activities.

The people of Arunachal have a varied repertoire of polyphonic music and folk songs. Folk dances, practiced from ancient times are still very popular among the different ethnic communities of Arunachal Pradesh. For instance, the dance of the Noctes called the Mayang Mouli Tali or 'round dance' depicts the way of life of the Noctes. The racial dances of the Wancho tribe called the Cherioklal and Garthik are performed during special occasions.

Arunachal has more than 70 dialects, with 30 of them being deemed as 'minor languages'. Some of the most predominant languages are Monpa, Adi, Nyishi, Apatani,Sherdukpen and Tagin. The official language of Arunachal is English, but Hindi is also widely spoken in the state.

The state is well-known for its breathtaking natural settings and its lovely locations, such as the gushing mountain streams, beautiful alpine meadows and flowery orchards. There are several incredible spots for trekking, such as the Bomdila Monastery and the Tawang Monastery. The Madhuri Lake in Zemithang Valley and the snow-capped mountains of Hunga are some of the must-visit places in Arunachal Pradesh.

All in all, Arunachal Pradesh is a great place with vibrant cultures, distinct dialects, and spectacular places. Its intriguing traditions, linguistic richness and natural beauty are some of the main reasons why it is one of the most popular tourist destinations.

CHAPTER THREE

Assam

Assam is a state located in the northeastern region of India, known for its rich culture, traditions, and natural beauty. The state is home to diverse ethnic groups, each with their own unique customs, languages, and traditions.

The culture of Assam is heavily influenced by the Assamese people, the dominant ethnic group in the state. The state is known for its traditional dance forms, such as the Bihu and the Sattriya, which showcase the state's rich cultural heritage. Assam is also known for its traditional handicrafts, including silk products, and the exquisite Assam tea. The cuisine of Assam is characterized by its use of local herbs and spices, with popular dishes like fish curry, dhekia xaak aru bhaji and pitha being enjoyed by locals and tourists alike.

The state is home to many important historical and religious sites, including the Kamakhya Temple, the Sivasagar, and the Hajo. Assam is also known for its natural beauty, with popular tourist destinations such as the Kaziranga National Park, the Manas National Park and the Dibru-Saikhowa National Park.

The official language of Assam is Assamese, while other languages spoken in the state include Bengali, Bodo and Hindi. The majority of the population follows Hinduism, but there is also a significant presence of Islam, Buddhism, and Christianity in the state.

Assam is a state that offers a unique blend of culture, traditions, and natural beauty. It is an ideal destination for those interested in exploring the diversity of India's culture, as well as for nature enthusiasts looking to explore the state's beautiful landscapes and national parks.

CHAPTER FOUR

Bihar

Bihar is a state located in the eastern region of India, known for its rich history, culture, and religious significance. The state is home to diverse ethnic groups, each with their own unique traditions, customs, and languages.

The culture of Bihar is heavily influenced by the Hindu and Buddhist religions, with many festivals and rituals being celebrated throughout the year. The state is also known for its traditional handicrafts, including Madhubani paintings, tussar silk, and stone and terracotta carvings. The cuisine of Bihar is characterized by its simplicity, with popular dishes like litti chokha, sattu, and fish curry being enjoyed by locals and tourists alike.

The state is home to many important religious and historical sites, including the Mahabodhi Temple, the Bodhi Tree, and the Nalanda University. Bihar is also known for its natural beauty, with popular tourist destinations such as the Valmiki National Park, the Bhimbandh Wildlife Sanctuary and the Vikramshila Gangetic Dolphin Sanctuary.

The official language of Bihar is Hindi, while other

languages spoken in the state include Magahi, Bhojpuri and Angika. The majority of the population follows Hinduism, but there is also a significant presence of Buddhism, Jainism and Islam in the state.

Bihar is a state that offers a unique blend of culture, history, and religion. It is an ideal destination for those interested in exploring the rich cultural heritage of India, as well as for those looking to experience the state's natural beauty and wildlife.

CHAPTER FIVE

Chattisgarh

Chhattisgarh, located in central India, is a culturally vibrant state with traditional arts and culture that has been passed down from generation to generation. The state is known for its festivals and colorful, expansive artistry. Language, traditions, and places in Chhattisgarh are integral parts of the state as they are the source of its unique identity in the country.

Language is an important part of Chhattisgarh's culture, as it is the primary marker of its unique identity. Chhattisgarhi, the native language of the state, is an Indo-Aryan language related to Hindi and Marathi. It is spoken by nearly 18.6 million people and is used by other languages such as Jharkhand and Bihar. Chhattisgarhi also has a separate script known as "Devanagari" which is derived from the Sanskrit language. Other languages also spoken in the state include Bhilali, Dhankari, and Halbi.

Traditions are deeply embedded in the culture of Chhattisgarh. They are often celebrated through festivals like Diwali, Navratri, and Dusshera, which commemorate the victories of gods and goddesses. The state also has another traditional festival called "Rajim" which is celebrated to mark the onset of spring. The region is also known for its folk dances and music. The most popular one is the Panthi or Panthini dance, which is performed throughout the state.

Chhattisgarh is home to a vast array of places of worship and spiritual sites. The largest and most famous of these is the Shiva temple in the Mahendra Bhawan district. The area is also home to several other Jain temples, as well as a few Buddhist ones. Other important sites of worship in Chhattisgarh include the Mata Dwarkamai temple in the Basantpur district and the Mahamaya temple in the Gudha district.

Chhattisgarh is home to a number of historically important places. These include the Bhoramdeo temple, the Kota Shriramshanka temple, the Kalibangan fort, the Ratanpur fort and many more. These places are popular tourist destinations and are much loved by locals and visitors alike.

In conclusion, language, traditions, and places are integral to Chhattisgarh's cultural identity, bringing together the colorful and historically significant aspects of the state. With its vibrant cultural diversity and many places of worship and historical sites, Chhattisgarh is a vibrant and exciting destination.

CHAPTER SIX

Goa

Goa is a state located on the western coast of India, known for its beautiful beaches, rich culture, and unique history. The state was a Portuguese colony for over 450 years, and this has had a significant influence on Goa's culture, language, and architecture.

The culture of Goa is a blend of Indian and Portuguese influences. The state is known for its traditional dance forms, such as the Goa Folk Dance and the Konkani Song, which showcase the state's rich cultural heritage. Goa is also known for its traditional handicrafts, including the famous Goan pottery and the hand-painted tiles. The cuisine of Goa is characterized by its use of local seafood and spices, with popular dishes like vindaloo, fish curry and bebinca being enjoyed by locals and tourists alike.

The state is home to many important historical and religious sites, including the Old Goa churches, the Fort Aguada and the Dudhsagar waterfall. Goa is also known for its natural beauty, with popular tourist destinations such as the Baga, Anjuna, and Colva beaches.

The official language of Goa is Konkani, while other

languages spoken in the state include Hindi, English and Marathi. The majority of the population follows Hinduism, but there is also a significant presence of Christianity in the state.

Goa is a state that offers a unique blend of culture, traditions, and history. It is an ideal destination for those interested in exploring the diversity of India's culture, as well as for beach enthusiasts looking to enjoy the state's beautiful beaches and nightlife.

CHAPTER SEVEN

Gujarat

Gujarat is an Indian state rich in cultures, traditions, languages, and places. Within its boundaries lie Gujarat's ports, hill stations, and shrines that offer a peek into the cultural history and heritage of the Gujarati people. Gujarat is a state located in western India with a rich and vibrant history and culture. Gujarat is the birthplace of Mahatma Gandhi, the father of the nation, and is home to many diverse cultures and religions. Gujarati is the official language of Gujarat, and is spoken by the majority of the population.

Gujarat's culture is an amalgamation of several ethnicities, each boasting its own unique customs. The Gujarati language, an Indo-Aryan language, is the primary language of the state and is spoken by the majority of the population. The distinctive, traditional Gujarati culture is a melting pot of various traditions and beliefs, such as Hinduism, Jainism, Sikhism, and Islam. However, despite this cultural diversity, the Gujaratis share a unique bond of friendship, respect, hospitality, and kindness, which are the basis of a strong, prosperous society.

The traditional Gujarati food is usually vegetarian, but

Marwari and other minority cultures can often be seen serving non-veg food. Gujarati cuisine is full of flavor and variety, with different regions of the state having their own flavors and ingredients. Gujarati's love to cook and serve food with love and generosity.

Gujarati people are among the most colorful of India's population and follow different rituals and customs depending on their religion. Notable festivals, such as Diwali, Holi, and Navratri, are celebrated in true Gujarati style, with celebrations lasting for days and nights. Women dress in bright and vibrant traditional saris, and sleek, traditional salwar kameez and colourful cultural performances are aplenty.

Gujarat is blessed with beautiful hill stations, vast deserts, and long coastlines that offer stunning scenic views. From the majestic view of the Aravali mountain range to the unrivalled beauty of the Gir National Park, the state has numerous places of interest that shall leave you in awe.

Gujarat is a diverse and vibrant state, which should be visited to enjoy and explore its incredible culture, traditions, language, and places. The friendly hospitality and the amazing local cuisine promise a fulfilling and unforgettable experience.

Gujarati is the language with a rich literary heritage and is known for its lyrical and melodic quality.

The culture of Gujarat draws from a long history and is deeply rooted in its traditions and customs. Music, dance and literature form an important part of the culture and are often used to express emotion and tell stories. Gujarati cuisine is characterized by its use of spices, vegetables, grains and pulses, which are all cooked in a variety of ways. Popular dishes include dhokla, thepla, and khandvi.

Gujarat is also known for its handcrafted items, such as textiles, jewelry, pottery and wooden furniture. The craftsmanship and skill of traditional craftsmen is highly celebrated and appreciated. Gujarat has a rich heritage and a vibrant culture that is unique and distinct.

It is a place that celebrates its diversity and embraces its traditions and customs, making it an incredibly special and beautiful place to visit.

CHAPTER EIGHT

Haryana

Haryana is a small state in North India and is known for its rich culture, diverse traditions and vibrant languages. This state is home to some of the renowned historical places and is an important part of India.

Haryana is known for its vibrant culture and rich history. Some of its great aspects are its festivals, its cuisine, its clothes and its traditional music and dance. The festivals of Haryana include the popular Holi, Diwali and Haryana Suraj Festival. The music and dance form here include bhajans and folk songs, which are enjoyed by everyone. The state is also known for its colourful traditional clothes called 'dhoti Kurta', which is worn by both men and women. The cuisine of Haryana is known for its dishes made from lentils and curd, along with other popular snacks such as Singari, Bhaturc and Kulhad wali dal.

Haryana is also known for its diverse traditions, which include many rituals and customs. Some of these customs are practised on different events such as marriages and birthdays. For example, in some parts of Haryana, traditional dance is used to celebrate the birth of a child. Similarly, women sing special songs to mark the start of the wedding season.

Haryana is also known for its vibrant language. The main language spoken here is Hindi, But people speak many other languages like Punjabi, English, and Haryanvi. Each language has its own unique vocabulary and slang words, which add to the variety of the language.

Haryana is home to many important and historical places. These include the city of Delhi and its surrounding cities, the ancient forts and palaces of Rajasthan and the religious sites of Haryana. One important place in Haryana is the historic Qutab Minar in Delhi, which is an impressive monument that stands tall in the city's skyline. Similarly, the City Palace in Jaipur, Rajasthan is also a famous tourist destination in Haryana.

Haryana is known for its vibrant culture, diverse traditions, and vibrant languages. It is home to many important and historical places that are visited by tourists from all over the world. Therefore, one must learn about the culture and traditions of Haryana to appreciate its beauty and charm.

CHAPTER NINE

Himachal Pradesh

Himachal Pradesh is a state located in the northern region of India, known for its picturesque landscapes, snow-capped mountains, and rich culture and traditions. The state is home to diverse ethnic groups such as the Paharis, Gaddis, and Kinners, each with their own unique customs and languages.

The culture of Himachal Pradesh is heavily influenced by the Hindu religion, with many festivals and rituals being celebrated throughout the year. The state is also known for its traditional handicrafts, including woolen shawls, wood carvings, and metal crafts. The cuisine of Himachal Pradesh is a blend of Indian and Tibetan influences, with popular dishes like dham, siddu, and chha gosht being enjoyed by locals and tourists alike.

The state is home to many important religious and historical sites, including the Jwalamukhi Temple, the Naina Devi Temple, and the Bhimakali Temple. The state is also known for its natural beauty, with popular tourist destinations such as the Kullu Valley, the Shimla Hills, and the Kinnaur Valley.

The official language of Himachal Pradesh is Hindi, while other languages spoken in the state include Pahari, Kinnauri, and English. The majority of the population follows Hinduism, but there is also a significant presence of Buddhism in the state.

Himachal Pradesh is a state that blends natural beauty, cultural heritage and religious diversity. It is an ideal destination for those interested in exploring the diversity of India's culture and traditions, as well as nature enthusiasts looking to explore the state's beautiful landscapes.

CHAPTER TEN

Jharkhand

Jharkhand is a state located in the eastern region of India, known for its rich culture, traditions, and history. The state is home to diverse ethnic groups, each with their own unique customs, languages, and traditions.

The culture of Jharkhand is heavily influenced by the tribal communities that make up a significant portion of the state's population. The state is known for its traditional dance forms, such as the Chhau and the Karma, which showcase the state's rich cultural heritage. Jharkhand is also known for its traditional handicrafts, including bamboo and bell metal craft. The cuisine of Jharkhand is characterized by its use of local herbs and spices, with popular dishes like dhuska, chira and arsa being enjoyed by locals and tourists alike.

The state is home to many important historical and religious sites, including the Parasnath Hill, the Rajrappa Temple and the Jonha falls. Jharkhand is also known for its natural beauty, with popular tourist destinations such as the Betla National Park, the Palamu Tiger Reserve and the Dassam falls.

The official language of Jharkhand is Hindi, while other languages spoken in the state include Santhali, Bengali and Odia. The majority of the population follows Hinduism, but there is also a significant presence of Buddhism, Christianity, and Animism in the state.

Jharkhand is a state that offers a unique blend of culture, traditions, and history. It is an ideal destination for those interested in exploring the diversity of India's culture, as well as for nature enthusiasts looking to explore the state's beautiful landscapes and national parks.

CHAPTER ELEVEN

Karnataka

Karnataka is a state in India located at the Southernmost region. It is known for its diverse culture, traditions, language and places. Karnataka has many distinct cultural practices, most of which are derived from the Dravidian and traditional Indian influences. Furthermore, its language, Kannada, is a Dravidian language and serves as one of the main regional languages in India. Last but not least, the state is full of exciting places with a variety of things to explore.

Karnataka's culture is rich and varied, and is heavily based on Dravidian and Indian influences. One example of this is the traditional practice of weaving sarees with intricate patterns and vibrant colors, particularly in the areas near Mysore and Udupi. Traditional music and dance styles are also practiced, such as Yakshgana. This style is usually performed in theater-style and is often accompanied by a classical music orchestra. Different parts of Karnataka are also known for different types of martial arts, such as Malla-Yuddha, Kabaddi and Chukkara.

The language of Karnataka is Kannada, which is a Dravidian language spoken by the majority of people in the state. It has a long literary heritage, with literary works dating back to the 9th century. It is the official language of the state and is spoken by a majority of the population. Furthermore, it is one of the most popular languages in India and has been recognised by the Indian government as one of its official languages.

Karnataka is also an attractive tourist destination, with wonderful places to explore and different types of activities to enjoy. There are many famous historical sites like Hampi, Badami and the group of monuments at Pattadakal. Bijapur is another popular spot, which has the famous Gol Gumbaz and the Ibrahim Rauza which are some of the major Islamic monuments in India that showcase the Islamic architecture of the era. The beach towns of Udupi and Gokarna are some of the best spots to spend a weekend away!

In conclusion, Karnataka is a wonderful place to explore, with its diverse culture, traditions, language and places. From the intricate saree weaving in Udupi to the beautiful monuments in Bijapur, there are lots of interesting things to discover in this state. Furthermore, Kannada is an important language in India and one of the official languages of the state. The culture, traditions, language and places of Karnataka are a fascinating representation of the history and heritage of this wonderful place.

CHAPTER TWELVE

Kerala

Kerala is a state located in the southern region of India, known for its rich culture, traditions, and history. The state is known for its diverse culture and heritage, which is reflected in its art, music, dance, and literature.

The culture of Kerala is heavily influenced by the Hindu, Muslim and Christian religion, with many temples, churches, mosques, festivals and rituals being an integral part of the state's culture. The state is known for its traditional dance forms, such as the Kathakali and the Mohiniyattam, which showcase the state's rich cultural heritage. Kerala is also known for its traditional handicrafts, including Kathakali masks, coir products, and the famous golden filigree jewellery. The cuisine of Kerala is characterized by its use of local herbs and spices, with popular dishes like dosa, idli, and sambhar, as well as traditional Kerala dishes such as appam, dosa, idli and sambar and the world-renowned sea food.

The state is home to many important historical and religious sites, including the Padmanabhaswamy Temple, the Guruvayur Temple, and the Jewish Synagogue. Kerala is also known for its natural beauty, with popular tourist destinations such as the backwaters, the hill stations and the beaches.

The official language of Kerala is Malayalam, while other languages spoken in the state include English, Hindi and Tamil. The majority of the population follows Hinduism, but there is also a significant presence of Islam and Christianity in the state.

Kerala is a state that offers a unique blend of culture, traditions, and history. It is an ideal destination for those interested in exploring the diversity of India's culture, as well as for nature enthusiasts looking to explore the state's beautiful landscapes and natural wonders. The state also has a rich literature and poetry, with Malayalam language being one of the oldest languages of India and has a rich history of literature, poetry, and plays. The state also has a rich tradition of classical dance and music. Overall, Kerala is a state that offers a unique blend of culture, tradition, and history, making it an ideal destination for tourists looking for a diverse and authentic experience."

CHAPTER THIRTEEN

Madhya Pradesh

Madhya Pradesh is a state located in the central region of India, known for its rich culture, traditions, and history. The state is home to diverse ethnic groups, each with their own unique customs, languages, and traditions.

The culture of Madhya Pradesh is heavily influenced by the Hindu religion, with many temples, festivals and rituals being an integral part of the state's culture. The state is known for its traditional dance forms, such as the Kathak and the Bhangra, which showcase the state's rich cultural heritage. Madhya Pradesh is also known for its traditional handicrafts, including tribal jewelry, bell metal craft, and the famous Madhubani paintings. The cuisine of Madhya Pradesh is characterized by its use of local herbs and spices, with popular dishes like poha, dal bafla and jalebi being enjoyed by locals and tourists alike.

The state is home to many important historical and religious sites, including the Khajuraho temples, the Sanchi Stupa and the Gwalior Fort. Madhya Pradesh is also known for its natural beauty, with popular tourist destinations such as the Kanha National Park, the Pachmarhi and the Bandhavgarh National Park.

The official language of Madhya Pradesh is Hindi, while other languages spoken in the state include Urdu and English. The majority of the population follows Hinduism, but there is also a significant presence of Islam and Buddhism in the state.

Madhya Pradesh is a state that offers a unique blend of culture, traditions, and history. It is an ideal destination for those interested in exploring the diversity of India's culture, as well as for history enthusiasts looking to explore the state's rich heritage and landmarks.

CHAPTER FOURTEEN

Maharashtra

Maharashtra, the third largest and second most populous state in India, is one of the most diverse and culturally rich states in the country. This diversity is reflected in many aspects of life, including its culture, traditions, language, and places.

A major part of Maharashtra's culture can be seen in its traditional festivals and celebrations. Ganesh Chathurthi is considered the most important festival and is celebrated with much fanfare across the state. Other important festivals are Gudi Padwa, Makar Sankranti, and Shiv Jayanti. People also celebrate their own local festivals that reflect their unique cultural traditions. Holi or 'Rang Panchami', for example, is widely celebrated in rural parts of the state with much enthusiasm and zeal.

Maharashtra's cultural traditions are also deeply embedded in its language. Marathi is the official language of Maharashtra and is spoken by over seventy percent of its population. Marathi is frequently used in literature, film, music, and other forms of art. It also is an important language for cultural expressions such as storytelling and regional folklore.

Apart from its culture, Maharashtra is also well known for its plethora of tourist destinations. Tourists can find a wide range of interesting locations to explore in this western state of India. Major tourist spots include Mumbai, the state capital, Pune, the cultural hub of the state, and a number of world-famous hill stations such as Mahabaleshwar and Matheran. People can also explore picturesque beaches, national parks, sacred temples, and archaeological sites.

In summary, Maharashtra is a state which is well known for its rich and vibrant culture. This is reflected in its celebrations, traditions, language, and places. All of these aspects have contributed significantly to the vast cultural diversity and wonders that the state of Maharashtra offers.

CHAPTER FIFTEEN

Manipur

Manipur is a state located in the northeastern region of India, known for its rich culture, traditions, and natural beauty. The state is home to diverse ethnic groups, each with their own unique customs, languages, and traditions.

The culture of Manipur is heavily influenced by the Meitei people, the dominant ethnic group in the state. The state is known for its traditional dance forms, such as the Manipuri Ras Lila and the Pung Cholom, which showcase the state's rich cultural heritage. Manipur is also known for its traditional handicrafts, including bamboo and cane products, and textiles. The cuisine of Manipur is characterized by its use of local herbs and spices, with popular dishes like Chak-hao kheer, Chamthong, and Iromba being enjoyed by locals and tourists alike.

The state is home to many important historical and religious sites, including the Kangla Fort, the Shree Govindajee Temple, and the War Cemetery. Manipur is also known for its natural beauty, with popular tourist destinations such as the Dzukou Valley, the Keibul Lamjao National Park, and the Loktak Lake.

The official language of Manipur is Meiteilon, while other languages spoken in the state include Bengali, Hindi and English. The majority of the population follows Hinduism, but there is also a significant presence of Buddhism, Christianity and indigenous religious practices in the state.

Manipur is a state that offers a unique blend of culture, traditions, and natural beauty. It is an ideal destination for those interested in exploring the diversity of India's culture, as well as for nature enthusiasts looking to explore the state's beautiful landscapes and national parks.

CHAPTER SIXTEEN

Meghalaya

Meghalaya, situated in the North East of India, is one of seven states that form the northeast region. Comprising of the Garo, Khasi, and Jaintia Hills, it is known for its rich and diverse culture and traditions, which has been handed down through generations.

The most prominent among the traditional cultures of Meghalaya are the customs of the Garo tribe, belonging to the Bodo-Kachari group. Common cultural practices of the Garo include nature worship and the performance of rituals such as those related to ancestor worship and the traditional medicine.

The Khasi society is organized deeply with the roles of men and women clearly defined. This society values education, and places importance on female education and the right to inherit property. Folk dances and music are a major component of Khasi culture and traditions. Music, as well as dancing, is seen as a way to drive away evil, while folk songs portray the day-to-day life of people.

Meghalaya is also known for a diverse language. The official language of Meghalaya is English, while many other languages are also spoken, including Khasi, Garo, and Sanskrit. Aside from these, Hindi and other local languages are also widely used.

Meghalaya's rich and diverse culture is reflected in its many places of worship. . Meghalaya is home to numerous Hindu temples, Christian churches, Buddhist temples and other forms of religious places that serve as pilgrimage centers for the locals.

In addition, Meghalaya is known for its natural beauty. From the Nokrek Biosphere Reserve to the beautiful temples spread across the state, Meghalaya has a lot to offer to its visitors. With its exotic flora and fauna, hilly terrains and picturesque scenes, it is no wonder why the state is often referred to as the "abode of clouds".

Meghalaya is well known for its diverse culture, traditions, language as well as its rich natural beauty. With its unique culture, language, and places of worship, Meghalaya is sure to have something for everyone.

CHAPTER SEVENTEEN

Mizoram

Mizoram is a state located in the northeastern region of India, known for its rich culture, traditions, and natural beauty. The state is home to diverse ethnic groups, each with their own unique customs, languages, and traditions.

The culture of Mizoram is heavily influenced by the Mizo people, the dominant ethnic group in the state. The state is known for its traditional dance forms, such as the Cheraw and the Khuallam, which showcase the state's rich cultural heritage. Mizoram is also known for its traditional handicrafts, including bamboo products, and textiles. The cuisine of Mizoram is characterized by its use of local herbs and spices, with popular dishes like bamboo shoot dishes, smoked meat and fish being enjoyed by locals and tourists alike.

The state is home to many important historical and religious sites, including the Mizoram State Museum, the Solomon's Temple, and the Reiek Tlang. Mizoram is also known for its natural beauty, with popular tourist destinations such as the Phawngpui National Park, the Vantawng falls, and the Murlen National Park.

The official language of Mizoram is Mizo, while other languages spoken in the state include English. The majority of the population follows Christianity, but there is also a significant presence of Hinduism, Buddhism, and indigenous religious practices in the state.

Mizoram is a state that offers a unique blend of culture, traditions, and natural beauty. It is an ideal destination for those interested in exploring the diversity of India's culture, as well as for nature enthusiasts looking to explore the state's beautiful landscapes and national parks.

CHAPTER EIGHTEEN

Nagaland

Nagaland is an province in India, located in the Northeastern region near the borders of Myanmar. Rich in culture, tradition, language, and unique places, it is one of the most unique states in India.

The culture of Nagaland is embedded in their folklore, tribe-specific traditions and customs, and the unity they strive to maintain while living together. It is expressed through the often vibrant clothing worn on different occasions, the traditional art forms that adorn the houses in villages, and the prevalent musics and chants which are popular among a majority of the locals. The various sub-tribes of the state celebrate a number of festivals throughout the year, each having a distinct cultural significance. These festivals range from harvesting to worshipping the ancestors, and in all of them, traditional music is an integral part of the celebration.

Nagaland has a colorful tradition, which reflects its tribal history. One such tradition is Moatsu, a three-day celebration that is held every year with singing and dancing in the honour of Tsungremmong, the God who is believed to bring prosperity to the state of Nagaland. Another important tradition is Kupheine, where people come together and enjoy the bounties of nature by harvesting the latest crops and feasting on the newly available food.

Nagaland is home to 17 major languages and a variety of dialects. Mekyong is the most widely spoken language and is part of the Tibeto-Burman family of languages. Other spoken languages like Konyak, Angami, and Ao, each with their own dialects and sub-dialects, are part of the greater linguistic infrastructure of Nagaland.

The residents of Nagaland are well-known for inhabiting truly unique places. From the ancient historic Hornbill Festival in Kisama Heritage Village, which showcases the stunning beauty of the state and its culture, to Naga Bazar, which provides visitors with a good selection of indigenous products from the various tribes, there are many places to explore. Then, of course, there is the city of Kohima, the capital of Nagaland. This scenic city envelopes the beauty of the state's culture and unique architecture.

Overall, the culture, tradition, language, and places of Nagaland are one of a kind and would definitely interest the average person. Its unique characteristics make it a fascinating place to visit and learn more about the distinctness of its local culture.

CHAPTER NINETEEN

Odisha

Odisha is a state located on the eastern coast of India, known for its rich culture, traditions, and history. The state is home to diverse ethnic groups, each with their own unique customs, languages, and traditions.

The culture of Odisha is heavily influenced by the Odia people, the dominant ethnic group in the state. The state is known for its traditional dance forms, such as the Odissi and the Chhau, which showcase the state's rich cultural heritage. Odisha is also known for its traditional handicrafts, including applique work, stone carving and the silver filigree work. The cuisine of Odisha is characterized by its use of local herbs and spices, with popular dishes like dalma, chhena poda and rasagolla being enjoyed by locals and tourists alike.

The state is home to many important historical and religious sites, including the Konark Sun Temple, the Lingaraj Temple and the Mukteswara Temple. Odisha is also known for its natural beauty, with popular tourist destinations such as the Chilika Lake, the Dhauli and the Udayagiri and Khandagiri Caves.

The official language of Odisha is Odia, while other languages spoken in the state include Hindi and English. The majority of the population follows Hinduism, but there is also a significant presence of Buddhism and Jainism in the state.

Odisha is a state that offers a unique blend of culture, traditions, and history. It is an ideal destination for those interested in exploring the diversity of India's culture, as well as for history enthusiasts looking to explore the state's rich heritage and landmarks.

CHAPTER TWENTY

Punjab

Punjab is a state located in the northern region of India, known for its rich culture, history, and agriculture. The state is home to diverse ethnic groups, each with their own unique traditions, customs, and languages.

The culture of Punjab is heavily influenced by the Sikh religion, with many festivals and rituals being celebrated throughout the year. The state is also known for its traditional handicrafts, including phulkari embroidery, jutti shoes, and wood carvings. The cuisine of Punjab is rich and diverse, with popular dishes like makki di roti, sarson da saag, and tandoori chicken being enjoyed by locals and tourists alike.

The state is home to many important religious and historical sites, including the Golden Temple, the Jallianwala Bagh, and the Partition Museum. The state is also known for its agricultural heritage, with the state of Punjab being one of the leading producers of wheat, rice, and sugarcane in India.

The official language of Punjab is Punjabi, while other languages spoken in the state include Hindi and English.

The majority of the population follows Sikhism, but there is also a significant presence of Hinduism and Islam in the state.

Punjab is a state that is rich in culture, history, and heritage. It is an ideal destination for those interested in exploring the diverse culture and traditions of India, as well as for those looking to experience the state's rich agricultural heritage.

CHAPTER TWENTY-ONE

Rajasthan

Rajasthan is a state located in the northwest region of India, known for its rich history, culture, and architecture. The state is home to diverse ethnic groups, each with their own unique traditions, customs, and languages.

The culture of Rajasthan is heavily influenced by the Rajputs, a Hindu warrior clan who have played a significant role in the state's history. The state is known for its vibrant festivals and fairs, such as the Pushkar Camel Fair and the Mewar Festival, which showcase the state's rich cultural heritage. Rajasthan is also known for its traditional handicrafts, including blue pottery, wooden furniture, and textiles. The cuisine of Rajasthan is characterized by its use of spices, with popular dishes like dal bati churma, kachoris, and laal maas.

The state is home to many important historical and architectural sites, including the Amber Fort, the City Palace, and the Jantar Mantar. Rajasthan is also known for its natural beauty, with popular tourist destinations such as the Thar Desert, the Sariska National Park and the Keoladeo National Park.

The official language of Rajasthan is Hindi, while other languages spoken in the state include Rajasthani and English. The majority of the population follows Hinduism, but there is also a significant presence of Jainism and Islam in the state.

Rajasthan is a state that offers a unique blend of culture, history, and architecture. It is an ideal destination for those interested in exploring the rich cultural heritage of India, as well as for those looking to experience the state's natural beauty and wildlife.

CHAPTER TWENTY-TWO

Sikkim

Sikkim is a tiny landlocked state situated in the Himalayan Mountains in India. It is home to a wide range of cultures, traditions, languages, and places which contribute to its uniqueness compared to other places in the country.

The culture of Sikkim has been shaped by centuries of contact between the various ethnic and regional groups in the area. The predominant religion is Hinduism, with Buddhism, Christianity, Sikhism, and other faiths also present. These religions share not only different spiritual beliefs, but also specific practices and festivals. For example, Hindus celebrate Dusshera, Buddhism Sikkim's largest festival 'Gangtok Tanze', as well as Losar, and Christianity's Christmas and Good Friday. These religious festivals bring together the diverse communities in Sikkim and foster friendly relations.

Sikkim also has a distinct traditional art and architectural style that says a great deal about the people and their culture. Wooden structures, terracotta art, and the historic Buddhist monasteries are all symbols of Sikkim traditional architecture. There is also a wide variety of traditional clothing, ranging from the Namdha Shawls which are made from hand-spun and hand-woven wool to the traditional Nepali Dhaka Topi and Cholapato which are worn by both men and women.

The many languages spoken in Sikkim are testament to the different cultures and people it is home to. For example, Nepali is the official language of the state due to its large Nepali speaking population, while Hindi, Tibetan, Bhutia, Lepcha and English are also widely spoken.

Many of the places of Sikkim are also connected to its culture and history. The Chorten at Chardham Temple and the Rumtek Monastery are two of Sikkim's most important and significant sites. The former is a spiritual site associated with Tibetan Buddhism and the latter is the largest Tibetan Buddhist monastery outside of Tibet. The ancient Buddhist caves of Lachung and the ancient Tibetan Stupas of Kalimpong are other fascinating places to explore in Sikkim.

In conclusion, Sikkim is a place of immense culture, traditions, language and places. Its vibrant culture, diverse languages and religions and fascinating places provide visitors with an unforgettable experience.

CHAPTER TWENTY-THREE

Tamil Nadu

Tamil Nadu is a state located in the southern region of India, known for its rich culture, traditions, and history. The state is known for its ancient culture and heritage, which is reflected in its art, music, dance, and literature.

The culture of Tamil Nadu is heavily influenced by the Hindu religion, with many temples, festivals and rituals being an integral part of the state's culture. The state is known for its traditional dance forms, such as the Bharatanatyam and the Koothu, which showcase the state's rich cultural heritage. Tamil Nadu is also known for its traditional handicrafts, including Kanchipuram silk sarees, bronze sculptures and the famous Thanjavur paintings. The cuisine of Tamil Nadu is characterized by its use of local herbs and spices, with popular dishes like dosa, idli, and sambhar being enjoyed by locals and tourists alike.

The state is home to many important historical and religious sites, including the Meenakshi Amman Temple, the Brihadeeswarar Temple and the Kapaleeswarar Temple. Tamil Nadu is also known for its natural beauty, with popular tourist destinations such as the Ooty, Kodaikanal and the Yercaud.

The official language of Tamil Nadu is Tamil, while other languages spoken in the state include English and Hindi. The majority of the population follows Hinduism, but there is also a significant presence of Islam, Christianity and Buddhism in the state.

Tamil Nadu is a state that offers a unique blend of culture, traditions, and history. It is an ideal destination for those interested in exploring the diversity of India's culture, as well as for nature enthusiasts looking to explore the state's beautiful landscapes and natural wonders. The state also has a rich literature and poetry, with Tamil language being one of the oldest languages of India and has a rich history of literature, poetry, and plays. The state also has a rich tradition of classical dance and music. Overall, Tamil Nadu is a state that offers a unique blend of culture, tradition, and history, making it a perfect destination for those looking to experience the diversity of India.

KANYAKUMARI

Kanyakumari is a city located in the state of Tamil Nadu, India. It is situated 90 kilometres (56 mi) south of Thiruvananthapuram city, and about 20 kilometres (12 mi) south of Nagercoil, the headquarters of Kanniyakumari district. It is popular because it is the only places on earth where you can see the Sun Rise and Sun Set from the ocean. It is also the only place in India where one can enjoy the unique spectacle of Sunset and Moonrise simultaneously on full moon days.

The city is home to a 3000-year-old temple dedicated to

Goddess Kanniyakumari (the virgin Goddess), after which the town is named. The city has a population of 19,739, consisting of 9,884 males and 9,855 females, with a sex ratio of 997. It is served by the Metrorail, Metromover, and Metrobus services. Tourists can also take advantage of the city's extensive free trolley service.

The district was part of the princely state of Travancore during the colonial times prior to India's independence. You can also apply for hunting Licenses through the official Texas Parks & Wildlife Department website.

CHAPTER TWENTY-FOUR

Telengana

Telangana is a state located in the southern region of India, known for its rich culture, traditions, and history. The state was formed in 2014, as the 29th state of India, carved out of Andhra Pradesh. Telangana has a rich cultural heritage, which is reflected in its art, music, dance, and literature.

The culture of Telangana is heavily influenced by the Hindu religion, with many temples, festivals and rituals being an integral part of the state's culture. The state is known for its traditional dance forms, such as the Bathukamma and the Bonalu, which showcase the state's rich cultural heritage. Telangana is also known for its traditional handicrafts, including Pochampally ikat, Kondapalli toys and the famous Telangana pearl jewellery. The cuisine of Telangana is characterized by its use of local herbs and spices, with popular dishes like biryani, dosa and Telangana-style pickles being enjoyed by locals and tourists alike.

The state is home to many important historical and religious sites, including the Thousand Pillar Temple, the Warangal Fort, and the Salarjung Museum. Telangana is also known for its natural beauty, with popular tourist destinations such as the Kuntala Waterfall, the Pochera

Waterfalls and the Kawal Wildlife Sanctuary.

The official language of Telangana is Telugu, while other languages spoken in the state include Hindi, Urdu and English. The majority of the population follows Hinduism, but there is also a significant presence of Islam in the state.

Telangana is a state that offers a unique blend of culture, traditions, and history. It is an ideal destination for those interested in exploring the diversity of India's culture, as well as for history and nature enthusiasts looking to explore the state's rich heritage and natural beauty. The state is also known for its unique festivals, such as the Bathukamma and the Bonalu, which are celebrated with great enthusiasm and are a great way to experience the local culture and traditions. The state also has a rich literature and poetry, with Telugu language being one of the oldest languages of India and has a rich history of literature, poetry, and plays. Overall, Telangana is a state that offers a unique blend of culture, tradition, and history, making it a perfect destination for those looking to experience the diversity of India.

CHAPTER TWENTY-FIVE

Tripura

Tripura is a northeastern state of India. It is located at the northeastern corner of the country, surrounded by Bangladesh, Assam and Mizoram. Tripura has been the home to various ethnic and cultural groups since time immemorial. Its culture, traditions, language and places of Tripura make it an intriguing region that can fascinate any traveler.

Tripura's culture is an amalgamation of different communities living in harmony and peacefully interacting with each other. The state is home to various cultural elements like dance, music, handicrafts, paintings and sculpture. Tripura has several folk songs and dance forms such as Jhum, Lai Haraoba, Bihu and Hojagiri that are still preserved in the state and are represented in various cultural gatherings. The dance style, as well as the music, display an aspect of Tripura's cultural identity, and depict the stories of the gods and goddesses of the region.

Tripura also has various traditional ceremonies, rituals and festivals that are celebrated with immense enthusiasm by the locals. Some of the important festivals are Pous Prasav, Hojagiri dance festival, Kharchi Puja and Tukai. The rituals observed in these festivals demonstrate the deep relationship that the inhabitants of the state often have with their deities and nature.

Tripura is a linguistically diverse state. The main language of the region is Kokborok, also known as Tripuri language. Apart from Kokborok, some of the other languages spoken in the state are Bengali, English, Manipuri and Hmar. All these languages provide a vivid portraiture of the cultural diversity in the state.

Tripura also boasts of being home to various scenic and historical places. Udaipur is the most popular among the attractions of Tripura, it is home to some of the oldest and most important temples and monuments in the region. Gomti Ghat is another attraction in the state, it is a riverside area where people often come to relax, spend quality time and go boating. The Unakoti hills, one of the most significant sites of the state, are home to some ancient rock carvings and bas-reliefs, which are believed to date back to 7th or 8th century.

The culture, traditions, language and places of Tripura have been an integral part of the region from time immemorial. Traversing these places as a traveler helps in getting a deeper understanding of the culture, customs and rituals of the region, and provides a unique perspective on vibrant and colorful Tripuri culture.

CHAPTER TWENTY-SIX

Uttarakhand

Uttarakhand is a state located in the northern region of India, known for its natural beauty, rich culture, and spiritual significance. The state is home to diverse ethnic groups, each with their own unique traditions, customs, and languages.

The culture of Uttarakhand is heavily influenced by the Hindu religion, with many festivals and rituals being celebrated throughout the year. The state is also known for its traditional handicrafts, including woolen shawls, wooden toys, and metal crafts. The cuisine of Uttarakhand is a blend of Indian and Tibetan influences, with popular dishes like aloo ke gutke, chainsoo, and bal Mithai being enjoyed by locals and tourists alike.

The state is home to many important religious and historical sites, including the Kedarnath Temple, the Badrinath Temple, and the Hemkund Sahib. The state is also known for its natural beauty, with popular tourist destinations such as the Nainital, the Mussoorie and the Jim Corbett National Park.

The official language of Uttarakhand is Hindi, while other

languages spoken in the state include Garhwali and Kumaoni. The majority of the population follows Hinduism, but there is also a significant presence of Buddhism in the state.

Uttarakhand is a state that blends natural beauty, cultural heritage, and spiritual significance. It is an ideal destination for those interested in exploring the diversity of India's culture and traditions, as well as for nature enthusiasts looking to explore the state's beautiful landscapes and national parks.

CHAPTER TWENTY-SEVEN

Uttar Pradesh

Uttar Pradesh, often known by its abbreviation UP, is one of the largest states in India, both for its population and for its geographical size. It is known for its diversity and is home to many different ethnic and cultural groups, each with its own unique culture, language, and customs. As such, in order to understand UP, one must explore its traditions, languages, and places of importance.

The culture of Uttar Pradesh reflects its strong roots in India's heritage. Many of the local traditions and festivals are rooted in the Vedic Vedic civilization, which has been celebrated by local communities for centuries. As a result, a large number of festivals are celebrated throughout the year in UP, such as Holi, Diwali, Uttarayan, and Janmashtami. Additionally, the culture of UP is also heavily influenced by Mughal rule, as many monuments were built during the dynastic period.

Apart from its culture, UP is also home to many different languages. UP is home to many dialects of Hindi, which is the official language of the state. Other local languages include Urdu, Punjabi, Karmali, Maithili, Bhojpuri, and Awadhi. Many of these languages are distinct to UP and are important in both preserving and showcasing the different cultural heritages of the state.

Lastly, Uttar Pradesh is home to many important places, each having their own unique history and significance. Amongst the most notable places is a 2500 years old city called Lucknow. It is known for its grandiose Islamic architecture and is home to some of the most beautiful monuments. Other important places include Agra, which is home to the Taj Mahal, Varanasi, where Gautam Buddha supposedly gave his first sermon, and Mathura, the birthplace of Lord Krishna.

Uttar Pradesh is a state that is full of culture, traditions, languages, and important places. Its vastness and diversity make it one of India's most beautiful states and a favorite destination for travelers. This is why it is important to understand its various cultures, languages, and places to get a full understanding of UP and its rich history.

CHAPTER TWENTY-EIGHT

West Bengal

West Bengal is a state located in the eastern region of India, known for its rich culture, traditions, and history. The state is home to diverse ethnic groups, each with their own unique customs, languages, and traditions.

The culture of West Bengal is heavily influenced by the Bengali people, the dominant ethnic group in the state. The state is known for its traditional dance forms, such as the Kathak and the Chhau, which showcase the state's rich cultural heritage. West Bengal is also known for its traditional handicrafts, including silk products, and the exquisite Bengali sweets. The cuisine of West Bengal is characterized by its use of local herbs and spices, with popular dishes like fish curry, dosa and luchi being enjoyed by locals and tourists alike.

The state is home to many important historical and religious sites, including the Victoria Memorial, the Howrah Bridge, and the Birla Planetarium. West Bengal is also known for its natural beauty, with popular tourist destinations such as the Sundarbans, the Darjeeling and the Dooars.

The official language of West Bengal is Bengali, while other languages spoken in the state include Hindi and English. The majority of the population follows Hinduism, but there is also a significant presence of Islam, Buddhism, and Christianity in the state.

West Bengal is a state that offers a unique blend of culture, traditions, and history. It is an ideal destination for those interested in exploring the diversity of India's culture, as well as for history enthusiasts looking to explore the state's rich heritage and landmarks.

Union Territories per https://knowindia.india.gov.in/states-uts/

1. Andaman and Nicobar Islands(Port Blair)
2. Chandigarh(Chandigarh)
3. Dadra and Nagar Haveli and Daman & Diu(Daman)
4. The Government of NCT of Delhi(Delhi)
5. Jammu & Kashmir - (Srinagar-S*, Jammu-W*)
6. Ladakh(Leh)
7. Lakshadweep(Kavaratti)
8. Puducherry(Puducherry)

CHAPTER TWENTY-NINE

The Andaman and Nicobar Islands

The Andaman and Nicobar Islands is a Union Territory of India, located in the Bay of Bengal. The islands are known for their natural beauty, with lush forests, clear beaches, and beautiful coral reefs.

The culture of the Andaman and Nicobar Islands is heavily influenced by the indigenous tribes that have lived there for thousands of years. The islands are home to several tribes, including the Great Andamanese, Onge, Jarwa, and Sentinalese, each with their own unique culture and customs. The islands also have a rich history, with many historical sites such as the Cellular Jail, which was used during the British colonial period to exile political prisoners.

The islands are also known for their natural beauty, with popular tourist destinations such as Havelock Island, Neil Island and Ross Island. There are also many opportunities for water sports such as snorkeling, scuba diving, and fishing.

The official language of the islands is Hindi and English, but many other languages are also spoken, including Bengali, Tamil, and Malayalam. The majority of the population follows Hinduism, but there is also a significant presence of Christianity and Islam in the islands.

The Andaman and Nicobar Islands offers a unique blend of culture, tradition, and natural beauty. It is an ideal destination for those interested in exploring the culture of the indigenous tribes, as well as for nature enthusiasts looking to explore the island's beautiful landscapes and coral reefs. The islands also have a rich history and culture that can be explored by visiting the various museums and historical sites on the islands. Overall, the Andaman and Nicobar Islands is a unique destination that offers a unique blend of culture, tradition, and natural beauty.

CHAPTER THIRTY

Chandigarh

Chandigarh is a Union Territory and the capital of the Indian states of Punjab and Haryana. It is a planned city, designed by the famous French architect Le Corbusier, and is known for its modern architecture, well-planned layout, and cleanliness.

The culture of Chandigarh is a blend of Punjabi and Haryanvi culture, with a strong influence of modern, urban culture. The city is known for its vibrant street food scene, with a variety of local delicacies available at street-side vendors and in traditional dhabas.

There are many important places to visit in Chandigarh such as the Rock Garden, an open-air sculpture garden made entirely of industrial and urban waste materials, the Rose Garden, which is the largest of its kind in Asia and the Sukhna Lake, a popular spot for boating and picnics.

The official language of Chandigarh is Hindi and Punjabi, but most of the people in the city also speak and understand English. The majority of the population follows Hinduism and Sikhism, but there is also a significant presence of Islam and Christianity in the city.

Chandigarh is a city that seamlessly blends tradition and modernity. It is a great destination for those interested in exploring the culture and tradition of Punjab and Haryana, as well as for architecture enthusiasts looking to explore the city's famous modernist architecture. The city also has a good number of museums, art galleries and open spaces which make it an interesting destination for those interested in art and history. Overall, Chandigarh is a unique destination that offers a blend of culture, tradition, and modernity.

CHAPTER THIRTY-ONE

Dadra and Nagar Haveli and Daman and Diu

Dadra and Nagar Haveli and Daman and Diu is a Union Territory located on the western coast of India. It is made up of two separate geographical entities, Dadra and Nagar Haveli, and Daman and Diu.

The culture of Dadra and Nagar Haveli and Daman and Diu is heavily influenced by the history of the region, which has been ruled by various dynasties and empires over the centuries. The area has a rich cultural heritage, with many historical monuments, temples, and churches to explore.

The region is also known for its natural beauty, with scenic mountains, beaches, and waterfalls. Some of the popular tourist destinations include the Dudhni waterfall, the Jampore Beach, and the Diu Fort.

The official language of Dadra and Nagar Haveli and Daman and Diu is Gujarati, Hindi, and English. The majority of the population follows Hinduism, but there is also a significant presence of Islam and Christianity in the region.

Dadra and Nagar Haveli and Daman and Diu is a unique destination that offers a blend of culture, tradition, and natural beauty. It is an ideal destination for those interested in exploring the history and culture of the region, as well as for nature enthusiasts looking to explore the region's beautiful landscapes and beaches. The region also has a rich cultural heritage and offers a great opportunity to explore the art, architecture, and cultural heritage of the region. Overall, Dadra and Nagar Haveli and Daman and Diu is a destination that offers a unique blend of culture, tradition, and natural beauty.

CHAPTER THIRTY-TWO

The Government of NCT of Delhi

Delhi, the capital city of India, is a mesmerizing combination of ancient heritage and modern culture. It is a city that celebrates the richness of its culture, traditions, language and places.

Delhi has a deep rooted history that is reflected in its culture and traditions. Its streets are lined with monuments depicting its ancient heritage, providing the people of Delhi a sense of pride and connection to their identity. They are passionate about their culture and express it through traditional art, festivals and food. Indians celebrate many festivals throughout the year, with special celebrations such as Diwali and Navratri. Apart from festivals, the people of Delhi also have some regional culture practices such as the practice of Karva Chauth, where married women fast and pray for the wellbeing of their husbands.

Delhi's culture is also reflected in its language. Hindi, the most spoken language in the city, is filled with words, expressions and traditions that have been in the city for centuries. It is the official language of Delhi and is deeply rooted in its culture. Along with Hindi, many other dialects are spoken in the city, including Bhojpuri, Awadhi and Urdu.

Delhi is also home to some of the most beautiful places in India. Its monuments are recognized all over the world, such as the Red Fort, Qutub Minar, Humayun's Tomb, India Gate, Jama Masjid and many more. These monuments not only serve as reminders of the nation's rich heritage, but also provide a stunning visual experience for tourists. The city is also known for its gardens and parks, including the Mughal Garden and Lodhi Garden. Delhi Zoo is one of the oldest and largest in the country and is a popular destination for locals and tourists alike.

Delhi is a city filled with culture, tradition, language and beauty. It is a city that celebrates its history and is a beacon of India's national identity. It is an example of many cultures living in harmony, making it a beautiful and vibrant destination which is sure to captivate people of all backgrounds.

CHAPTER THIRTY-THREE

Jammu & Kashmir

Jammu and Kashmir is a state located in the northern region of India and is known for its rich culture and history. The state is home to diverse ethnic groups, each with their own unique traditions, customs and languages.

The culture of Jammu and Kashmir is a blend of Hindu, Muslim and Buddhist influences. The state is known for its traditional handicrafts, including pashmina shawls, carpets, wood carvings, and paper mache items. The cuisine of Jammu and Kashmir is also a reflection of its diverse culture, with dishes like rogan josh, dum aloo, and haak being popular among locals and tourists alike.

The state is home to many important religious and historical sites, including the Vaishno Devi Temple, the Amarnath Cave, and the Shankaracharya Temple. Jammu, the winter capital of the state, is known for its old temples and palaces, such as the Raghunath Temple and the Mubarak Mandi Palace. Srinagar, the summer capital of the state, is famous for its beautiful gardens and lakes, such as the Dal Lake and the Nishat Bagh.

The official language of Jammu and Kashmir is Urdu, while

other languages spoken in the state include Kashmiri, Dogri, Hindi, and English. The majority of the population is Muslim, but there is also a significant Hindu and Buddhist minority. The state is known for its unique blend of Hindu and Muslim cultures and customs, with festivals like Eid-ul-Fitr and Diwali being celebrated with equal fervor.

Jammu and Kashmir has a rich cultural heritage that has been shaped by centuries of history and the influences of various ethnic groups. The state is an ideal destination for those interested in exploring the diversity of India's culture and traditions.

CHAPTER THIRTY-FOUR

Ladakh

Ladakh Leh (summer), Kargil (winter)

Ladakh is a Union Territory located in the northernmost region of India. It is known for its unique culture and traditions, which are heavily influenced by Tibetan Buddhism. The official language is Ladakhi, but other languages such as Urdu, Hindi, and English are also widely spoken.

Leh, the summer capital of Ladakh, is known for its stunning landscapes and ancient Buddhist monasteries, such as the Leh Palace and the Thiksey Monastery. The city is also famous for its traditional festivals, such as the Ladakh Festival and the Hemis Festival, which showcase the region's rich cultural heritage.

Kargil, the winter capital of Ladakh, is known for its rugged mountain landscapes, and traditional culture. The city is known for its unique culture, which is heavily influenced by Buddhism and the ancient Bon religion. The city is also known for its traditional festivals, such as the Kargil Festival, which celebrates the region's rich cultural heritage.

Ladakh is also known for its natural beauty, including the Himalayan mountain ranges, the Indus River, and the Zanskar and Nubra Valleys. The region is also home to several ancient Buddhist monasteries, such as the Alchi Monastery, the Likir Monastery, and the Lamayuru Monastery, which are popular tourist destinations. Additionally, The region is also known for its trekking, mountaineering, and adventure sports opportunities.

CHAPTER THIRTY-FIVE

Lakshadweep

Lakshadweep is a Union Territory located in the Arabian Sea, off the coast of the Indian state of Kerala. It is made up of 36 small islands, of which only 10 are inhabited. The islands are known for their pristine beaches, coral reefs, and unique marine biodiversity.

The culture of Lakshadweep is heavily influenced by its geography and history. The islands have a rich history, with evidence of human habitation dating back to the Neolithic era. The islands have been ruled by various dynasties and empires over the centuries, and this is reflected in the architecture, art, and culture of the region.

The official language of Lakshadweep is Malayalam, but the majority of the population also speaks and understands Hindi, English, and Mahi. The majority of the population is Muslim, but there is also a significant presence of Hinduism and Christianity in the region.

The most important places to visit in Lakshadweep are the coral reefs, beaches, and marine national parks. Some of the popular tourist destinations include the Kadmat Island, Minicoy Island, and Agatti Island.

Lakshadweep is a unique destination that offers a blend of culture, tradition, and natural beauty. It is an ideal destination for those interested in exploring the unique marine biodiversity of the region, as well as for those interested in exploring the rich cultural heritage of the islands. The region is also a popular destination for water sports like scuba diving, snorkeling and sea walking. Overall, Lakshadweep is a destination that offers a unique blend of culture, tradition, and natural beauty, making it an ideal destination for those looking for a unique and memorable vacation experience.

CHAPTER THIRTY-SIX

Puducherry

Puducherry, part of the union territory of India, is a small but vibrant region with a unique culture and many captivating traditions, languages and places of interest.

For centuries, Puducherry was a colony of France and this long-standing colonial presence is obvious in its culture, which manages to maintain old-world charm while still embracing local Indian heritage. It has a fascinating mix of cultures that reflect its French, Tamil and Telugu history. This province of India showcases an exclusive seafood-based cuisine and a vibrant mix of traditional and modern music, theater and dance.

An important part of Puducherry's culture is its religious diversity. You can find Hindu, Christian and Muslim places of worship that all help define the fabric of the cultural scene. Alongside this, there are also several rituals and festivals unique to the region, such as the Car Street Fair, which is celebrated between the months of July and September.

The language spoken in this union territory, is Tamil; the official language is a mix of Tamil, French and English.

Bilingual signs featuring Tamil and English can be seen all around the city, such as in shops, educational and governmental institute. Other languages spoken in Puducherry include Telugu, Telopee and Urdu.

As for places of interest in Puducherry, tourists come from all over the world to explore this exciting region of India. Popular avenues of entertainment and relaxation include the beautiful beaches of India, such as the Paradise and Paradise beaches, both situated close to the sea. Another popular spot is the Sri Aurobindo Ashram, which is home to a collective of spiritual seekers and explores the themes of religion, philosophy, and spiritual sciences. Tourists also love to visit the Vivekananda and Cuddalore House, which was gifted to Swamy Vivekananda by the people of Pondicherry when he visited in December 1892. People interested in art can enjoy the ancient and modern architecture at the French Quarter, which is filled with colonial buildings, art galleries and cafes.

In summary, Puducherry is a vibrant region of India with an interesting culture, many captivating traditions, languages, and special places of interest. Blessed with French, Tamil, and Telugu heritage, it is a must-visit destination for those looking to explore a region of India that is rich in culture, language and history.

Other Books Of The Author

1. The Moments When I Met God
2. Kashiyile Theertha Pathangal
3. GURU GYAN VANI
4. Abhiprerak Gita
5. ASSI SE JAIN GHAT TAK
6. Hopelessness of Arjuna
7. The Soul and It's True Nature
8. Sense of Action (Karma)
9. Action through Wisdom
10. Action through Wisdom
11. THEORY AND PRACTICAL OF EVERY ACTION
12. LOGICAL UNDERSTANDING OF THE SUPREME
13. THE IMPERISHABLE SUPREME
14. Yatra Nishadraj se Hanuman Ghat Tak
15. Yatra Karnatak Ghat se Raja Ghat Tak
16. Yatra Pandey Ghat se Prayagraj Ghat Tak
17. Yatra Ranjendra Prasad Ghat se Dattatreya Ghat Tak
18. YaatraSindhiya Ghat se Gwaliar Ghat Tak
19. Yatra Mangala Gauri Ghat se Hanuman Gadhi Ghat Tak
20. Yatra Gaay Ghat Se Nishad Ghat Tak
21. MAA GANGA, GHATEN EVM UTSAV
22. Ganga Arti Dev Deepavali evam Any Utsav
23. Potentials of Digitalized India
24. VEDIC CONSCIOUSNESS
25. A Brief Introduction to Vedic Science
26. Kashi ke Barah Jyotirling
27. IMPACT OF MOTIVATION
28. Let's have a Milky Way Journey
29. Color Therapy in a Nutshell

30. Rigveda in a Nutshell
31. Yajurveda in a Nutshell
32. Samveda in a Nutshell
33. Atharva Veda in a Nutshell
34. Ayushman Bhava - Ayurveda
35. Srimad Bhagavad Gita and Upanishad Connection
36. Srimad Bhagavad Gita - an attempt to summarize each chapter.
37. Facts and Impact of Nakshatra
38. Astro Gems - NAVARATNA
39. Ekadashi - A Concise Overview
40. A Concise View of Hanuman Chalisa
41. Inspirational Gita
42. Nakshatraranyam
43. Summary of 18 Mahapuranas
44. Synopsis of 18 Upa Puranas
45. Rigvediya Upanishads
46. Shukla Yajurvediya Upanishads
47. Krishna Yajurvediya Upanishads
48. Samavediya Upanishads
49. Atharvavediya Upanishads
50. The Seven Great Sages
51. From Rocket Scientist to President Dr. APJ Abdul Kalam
52. The Visionary's Voice - Quotes of Dr. APJ Abdul Kalam
53. The Wisdom of Swami Vivekananda: Insights and Inspiration from a Legendary Spiritual Teacher
54. Ayurvedic Remedies from the Garden
55. Sages and Seers
56. Rising Strong – Motivational Stories of Women
57. Beyond Flames -Mystery stories of Funeral Ghat Manikarnika
58. The Origins of Tulsi: A Look at the Mythological Roots of the Plant"

59. The Holistic Cow: A Look at the Physical, Spiritual, and Cultural Importance of Cows in India
60. Arts of Healing
61. Exploring the Divine
62. Understanding Five Elements
63. The Etymology of Ram
64. Symbols of India
65. Voice of Change (About Speeches of Great Men)
66. She Speaks (About Speeches of Great Women)
67. Patriotism on Celluloid – Brief About Patriotic Films
68. The Music of Motivation: A Brief Guide to Inspirational Film Songs
69. Unlocking the Secrets of the Dashopanishads
70. A Cultural Mosaic
71. Ancient Traditions, Modern Minds
72. Ecos of Ancient Wisdom
73. Beneath the Surface
74. From Temples to Ashrams
75. Sages of the Subcontinent
76. The Art of Healling (Ayurveda, Yoga & Naturopathy)
77. Indian Kitchen
78. The Festivals of India
79. The Indian Epics Retold
80. The Power of Mantras
81. The Indian River Ganges
82. The Indian Architecture
83. Rites of Passage
84. The Indian Silk Road
85. The Indian Literature
86. The Indian Villages
87. The Indian Folks & Crafts
88. The Way of Buddha
89. The Ramayan of Tulsidas

90. Astrological Remedies
91. The Secret Power of Motivation
92. Secret of Developing your Inner Strength
93. The Secret Path to Motivation
94. The Art and Secret of Positive Thinking
95. The Secrets of Practicing Ethical Living
96. Indian Art and Painting
97. The Indian Herbalism
98. Bharatanatyam to Kathak
99. Exploring India's Astrological Remedies
100. The Indian Festival of Flowers
101. Indian Handicrafts
102. The Splashes of Joy – India's Colour Festival
103. The Indian Science of Astrology
104. The Indian Mythology
105. Path to Enlightenment
106. The Indian Spirituality for Children
107. Aromas of India
108. The Secrets of Healthy Relationships
109. Ancestral Ties
110. The Indian Street Food
111. Discovering America
112. The Indian Textile
113. Listening to Motivational Speeches
114. Taste of India
115. A Cultural Journey through Indian Nuptials
116. Motivational Quote for Change
117. Secret Strategies for Making Money
118. Secrets to Cultivate a Positive Mindset

Contact

DR. JAGADEESH PILLAI

PhD in Vedic Science

Four Times Guinness World Record Holder

Winner of Mahatma Gandhi Vishwa Shanti Puraskar and Global Peace Ambassador

Gemology, Astro & Vastu Consultant - Spiritual Counselor

Consultant for designing World Record Ideas

Efficient Tarot Card Reader

9839093003

myrichindia@gmail.com

drjagadeeshpillai@facebook

drjagadeeshpillai@instagram

jagadeeshpillai@youtube

www. JAGADEESHPILLAI.com

|| LOKAHA SAMASTHAHA SUKHINO BHAVANTU ||

Printed by Libri Plureos GmbH in Hamburg, Germany